FROM EMPLOYEE TO ENTREPRENEUR

FROM EMPLOYEE TO ENTREPRENEUR TRAIN YOUR MIND

 FROM EMPLOYEE TO ENTREPRENEUR

 FROM EMPLOYEE TO ENTREPRENEUR

INDEX

What's your mentality?

Examining the Dream

Learn to listen to customers

Be a good supplier

Find a Mentor and Trainer

Final thoughts

FROM EMPLOYEE TO ENTREPRENEUR

What's your mentality?

Many small business owners and entrepreneurs started out as employees. They worked for someone else. The point is, if you've been an employee for years, it can be hard to shake off the bonds of the employee's mentality.

What does this mean?

If you have an employee mentality, you are more likely to look to other people to tell you what to do. You will find it difficult to take responsibility for the success and failure of your effort.

As an employee, you have no say in how the business is run. You only work hard to prove your worth so you can keep working.

Which one are you?

If you are an entrepreneur or business owner, think very differently. Essentially, responsibility stops (and starts) with you. You are responsible for the success and failure of your effort. And you're the one who makes all the important decisions (including who to designate to make the smallest decisions!). To find out if you're thinking like an employee or an entrepreneur, take this quick test:

- Are your tasks/responsibilities limited to a subset of what it takes for your business to thrive?

- Does your lifestyle fit into your income?

If an economic setback occurs, is the budget reduced to accommodate the reduction in income?

- Do you constantly seek external advice to make decisions even on a day-to-day basis?

If you answered "yes" to most of these questions, you most likely have an employee mentality. Here's why those with an entrepreneurial mindset would answer "no".

 FROM EMPLOYEE TO ENTREPRENEUR

Are your tasks/responsibilities limited to a subset of what it takes for your business to thrive?

Entrepreneurs understand that they occasionally have to do things in their business that are "above" or "below" their level of competence.

Their mental attitude is if you have to do it, do it, and they are not opposed to rolling up their sleeves and getting their arms dirty.

Is your lifestyle based on your income?

Entrepreneurs will try to develop their business, expand their product line, and

 FROM EMPLOYEE TO ENTREPRENEUR

expand their services when economic downturns occur. They don't let themselves be or remain victims of tax conditions.

If there is a money mishap, is the budget reduced to accommodate the reduction in income?

Entrepreneurs first send payments for themselves. They focus on bringing the money that supports the lifestyle they want and invest the rest in their business. That said, they also know and accept the ephemeral sacrifices that may be necessary to achieve a goal.

Do you constantly seek outside advice to make decisions even on a day-to-day basis?

FROM EMPLOYEE TO ENTREPRENEUR

Entrepreneurs manage their time and take responsibility for their actions. While they may be looking for mentors to guide them toward expanded growth, they are in control of their day-to-day actions and don't need someone else to tell them what they should accomplish or push them to do it.

Let's look at a few more differences

Monday Mentality

- Employees fear Monday. (Or, whichever is the beginning day of their work week.)

- Employers are not forced to work for a week. They approach each day as a different opportunity to go after their dreams.

Not my problem mentality

- Employees have this mentality that they see everything at work, whether it's their problem or not.

- Employers see everything as their duty, as they own what is happening in their business.

Friday Mentality (Thank God it's Friday)

- Employees are always waiting for their days off.

- Entrepreneurs are always looking for ways to expand their business even when they are not "working", they are considering ways to expand their entrepreneurial talent. They are looking forward to it every day!

When will I get a mentality boost?

- Employees think increases should come according to the schedule, rather than according to their job.

- Employers rarely consider when they will receive a raise. They realize that the more they work to help others, the greater their reward.

FROM EMPLOYEE TO ENTREPRENEUR

Oh no, what about the mentality now?

- Employees meet with a "oh no" mentality.

- Entrepreneurs meet with a brain mentality. They realize that excellent ideas come out of these meetings.

There are many more mentalities we can compare. In fact, if a few have come to mind as you read this, write them down.

 FROM EMPLOYEE TO ENTREPRENEUR

Examining the Dream

There are many employees who yearn to be their own bosses, but fear what the future might hold if they owned businesses. I would like to advise that if you are among those individuals, you would do well to become a great employee first! I spent many years as an employee and was constantly found to be a model employee.

My employer bosses constantly gave me high ratings. As I go through the list of employee mentalities, I can tell you frankly that I didn't have those mentalities. I was a great employee!

FROM EMPLOYEE TO ENTREPRENEUR

If you have a desire to be on your own one day, going after your dreams as an entrepreneur, you can start now. Approach your occupation as if you owned the company you work for.

Carrying that ownership spirit will reward you at work and prepare you for the day when you can devote yourself to your own business. You can be an entrepreneur while you are still working. Having this spirit will excite you to go after your own efforts when you are not on your employer's watch.

Positive Mind and Productivity

You spend about a third of your life at work. If you're spending it with negative individuals, it may really affect and depress

you.

By stopping negative thoughts as they enter your ears and not letting them advances in your thoughts, you will be doing a great deal of work to stay positive in a negative situation and develop your business skills. Here are ways to prevent horrible situations at work from getting stuck.

Owning a life outside of your job

Keep acquaintances who have a good knowledge of reality and with whom you can share a life that has nothing to do with the work you do. Refuse to talk about your work outside of work hours, particularly if the environment is toxic, except when it comes to ideas for your own business.

Recognize that most of what happens at work and most of the negativism; even that which is directed at you, is not about you.

Think of the stress your colleagues face at work, at home and in their personal lives and understand that they are projecting and shifting their anger towards you and others around you as well. Remember that dealing with people is crucial to being an entrepreneur.

Refuse to let your colleagues' work addiction, ambitions, and selfish behavior seep into your system.

It's easy to start letting negative behavior get

in the way by agreeing to perspectives or taking sides. Rather, choose to rise above it all while remaining neutral.

Defend your thoughts; sooner or later they will become your reality.

Make sure that the negativism around you does not continue to play in your head. Put music on your desk at a reasonable volume if you think it helps you focus. Take breaks to collect your thoughts. Keep favorable reminders in quotes and pictures around your workspace about what you are trying to learn and accomplish.

Really think about your options for starting your journey as an entrepreneur.

Some bosses can be emotionally abusive; if the company's environment doesn't look like it's going to change, evaluate whether this really is the best place for you and ways you can start your own business soon.

You spend more than eight hours a day at your desk juggling calls, emails and correspondence. Anyway, the pile of paper on your messy desk keeps growing taller, you eat more in the office than at home, and yet you barely meet the deadlines.

Discover ways to stay away from time traps and improve existing procedures to be not only more productive at work, but much less stressed and to develop skills you can use in your own business.

Look at those who waste time

The standard culprits are instant messaging, Internet browsing, personal calls, and gossip with colleagues. Minutes spent in these wrong directions can turn into hours of wasted time and productivity. Determine the limits of these actions and discover ways to politely end conversations.

Limit Distractions and Interruptions

Schedule times to track and respond to mail, email, and voicemail. If possible, turn off instant messengers and don't answer personal calls while working on other tasks.

 FROM EMPLOYEE TO ENTREPRENEUR

Coordinate and prioritize

If you're constantly searching for items on your messy desktop, give yourself time to organize your files, tools, and computer. Save paper and electronic files in marked folders. On your PC, create shortcuts and favorites to help find items quickly and easily.

Use a single portable calendar to keep track of all meetings, dates, and deadlines.

Produce a schedule to start and finish a given task and stick to it. Start and finish tasks on time. A daily or weekly "to do" list can also be a useful tool to stay on track and stay productive.

Be honest with yourself about your strengths and weaknesses and then budget time and work accordingly. It may be helpful to do the things you least like first, as they may consume more time and you are more likely to finish more interesting activities.

Compose meeting agendas and stay within allotted time.

Ineffective meetings that are late are a major cause of lost productivity.

As you take notes, write down all key information, such as date, time, attendees, program elements, and action items. This could save enough time to guess later. If in doubt, document.

Learn how to use new and better tools to get the job done and spend some time learning how to use existing tools more efficiently.

Discover a coach or mentor or take a class in time management, organizational strategies and productive business communication.

Take breaks

This can seem contradictory when flooded. However, the "turning point" is when it is even more important to stay clear and focused. It is easy to make mistakes and when you feel flooded. In fact, the schedule bursts into your day if it is essential. Even a short walk around the building can clear your mind and reduce stress, which promotes productivity.

 FROM EMPLOYEE TO ENTREPRENEUR

Learn to listen to customers

Watch and learn from the people you work with because they often demonstrate the habits you need to have when you're living an entrepreneur's life, such as how to listen to customers.

Look at what people want

There's a lot of discussion about listening these days. Listening is one of the most important skills you can learn. If you are able to stop and listen to your customers, you are able to pave the way to continued business

success.

Listening requires paying attention and reacting to customers' needs and desires. If you want to have your own business, you have to practice the art of active listening.

It is not enough to react to customers. You have to be able to anticipate their needs. Listening to customers is about positioning your company to be the answer to the needs of the buyer, ideally before they even ask.

Listening is also about getting involved with your customers. This includes really spending time with them, exploring things that are important to them, studying magazines and books that are written for them, and being an authority on the things

 FROM EMPLOYEE TO ENTREPRENEUR

that matter to them.

Your business must have an ideal customer. This is the prototype of the perfect customer for you. You need to attract these kinds of customers, and the more customers that fit the ideal, the better. So it adds up that this is the kind of customer you should be paying attention to.

A customer is someone who has bought from you or the company you work for, but is also someone who can buy from you. You should treat customers, prospects, and the general public with the same respect. Anyway, you should spend your time listening to the people you love most as customers.

Listening can (and should) happen

anywhere. That said, you can perfect your listening using particular tools and strategies.

Offline, you should be conducting customer surveys and simply going out and talking to customers and people. Go to fairs and conferences that are also attended by your ideal clients. If there isn't one in your area, start one.

As your experience grows, you may want to think about making some presentations. This is an incredible way to meet people and get individuals to tell you about the problems they face.

Online, the openings are endless. You can listen on Twitter with the help of Twitter Search. You are able to crawl keywords and phrases across the web using Google Alerts.

Forums are a great place to listen. You can also produce your own listening messages with a blog or podcast. Sure, this is you talking, but it will also force you to explore and learn about your customers. And you are able to encourage dialogue and feedback from readers.

Be sure to listen to where customers are talking. If you will be able to find out where the ideal customers congregate, online and offline, then you also have to be there.

Active listening will help you understand and better connect with your customers. It will facilitate sales and marketing, as you will be able to position yourself fairly between customer and need.

Becoming a great listener will also make you love the people you want to reach. Everyone loves to be heard. So close that trap, save that profit and loss sheet for a minute and start exploring your customers' world.

FROM EMPLOYEE TO ENTREPRENEUR

Be a good supplier

We all bring value to the workplace; whether it's the work we inject as employees, or the products and services we sell in our business.

A major performance review may not be enough to guarantee a promotion or even to maintain your line of work. In addition, a high quality product or service may not be enough on its own.

Giving the first mentality

The value is in the eye of the beholder (think how much more you can pay for an umbrella

on a shower day). Workers who are easy to get along with and reliable with tasks will be more useful to your manager than someone who causes stress at team meetings and regularly fails to meet deadlines.

In addition, a product will be more useful to a consumer if its favorite celebrity endorses it, if it is for sale, or if it includes a contributed bonus.

At the same time, we're becoming insensitive to ads; we've become wary of bonus offers, sales increases, and add-ons. We look for authenticity; that's what we value today.

Given the growing rivalry in the labor market, workers have to establish their value to the company in order to get and maintain their lines of work, as well as to advance to higher positions and acquire customers when it comes to having an entrepreneurial mindset.

Many consumers are whipped and worried and guard their purchases with caution. On the other hand, we are in the midst of a virtual flood of sales offers (there is no deficit there).

Consumers are choosing the products and services they find most useful. It is absolutely necessary to maximize the perceived value of what is offered. But you also need to support yourself and your loved ones. So what do you do?

Look for things you can add to your products

and services that don't cost you much but are really useful, for example, a downloadable e-book or an attached CD.

Approach someone who has a complementary business that serves your market and ask them to provide an additional product or service. It's a win-win, because they get exposure to their customers and you get the extra value for your offer.

Add value to your product or service by including case studies and/or recommendations. Think about who can have the maximum level of "social capital" for your audience.

Typically it will be someone your potential customers can relate to as if they have similar challenges and conditions OR someone you can admire for having achieved what they are trying to achieve.

Once you consider ways to increase the perceived value of what you provide, put yourself in your customer's shoes. Is there anything about your product or service that you leave out, but other people find useful? If you're not sure, survey satisfied buyers and customers.

Workers and business owners, become essential to your team by demonstrating yourself as a connector. Listen to the issues that individuals require and reconcile them with the individuals, products or services that have them.

FROM EMPLOYEE TO ENTREPRENEUR

Naturally, do it for additional work projects and office tasks, but also for personal matters.

For example, if someone tells you about an impressive vacation spot, and someone else is planning their next trip, suggest that the two people talk about it.

Point out the added value you are already giving your clients. You may regularly find clues that everyone else misses. Don't just assume your customers will notice: point them out in an email or blog post.

In this saturated market, a competitive business market and a challenging economy, there's a chance that the cream will rise to the top. Be sure to remind individuals of its value; why you are the cream as an entrepreneur.

FROM EMPLOYEE TO ENTREPRENEUR

Find a Mentor and Trainer

A mentor is a person with more experience in business, or simply in life, who can help an entrepreneur sharpen his powers and advise him on how to pilot new challenges.

A mentor can be a great help to an entrepreneur in a wide range of situations, whether providing advice on business techniques, reinforcing his network crusades or acting confidently when his work-life balance becomes unsustainable. However, the first thing you should know when looking for a mentor is what you are looking for in the agreement.

What having a personal trainer is for your body, having a trainer can be for your mind. Using a coach seems to be the last way for some individuals to get ahead in today's gaga business world.

Learn from others

What can your mentor do for you? Determining what type of resource you need is an imperative first step in seeking mentors. Starting with a list is a good way to start. You may want someone who is a great listener, someone with social connections, someone with experience in, say, marketing, accessible person.

Ideally, you'll find a mentor with all of these characters, but the reality is that you may have to make some compromises. After you count the characters you're looking for in a mentor, divide that list into wants and needs.

The next step is to "do an informative interview with many candidates and then return to your standards so that you don't get surprised by the chemistry and stay focused on your business or personal reasons for needing a mentor. By judging a combination of the qualitative and quantitative properties of each of your likely mentors, a top candidate will appear.

Keep in mind that it can be advantageous to have more than one mentor. If you think you can monopolize too much of your mentor's time, then several mentors may be the answer.

FROM EMPLOYEE TO ENTREPRENEUR

The benefits of having multiple mentors is that you are able to get a wide variety of views and when you have many mentors at once, if you are sitting around a table, the synergy between the mentors really helps to move your thinking along.

How to discover a mentor:

Start with loved ones and friends - When looking for a mentor, start close to home. Very close to home. From time to time you can talk to your own relatives or friends, people you trust, people you know where you can sit down and say, 'Wow, what you feel about that?

Think of those in your extended network - If your friends and loved ones already give you enough unsolicited advice, and you don't think that's the route for you, the choices you have left are individuals who don't know you as well or don't know you at all.

How do you ask such a big commitment from a virtual stranger? The opening movement is to take possession of their network of contacts. A positive word from a common acquaintance can help a mentoring relationship get off to a good start.

Also, you shouldn't choose a mentor overnight, which means you should keep your antenna ready to spot potential mentors at conferences, trade shows, etc. Meeting with a future mentor in person helps build a relationship and you may want to wait until

that connection develops before dismissing the question.

Think of the total strangers - perhaps none of the individuals in your network seem very appropriate for you. Start doing some research. Profiles of business owners in magazines and newspapers can be the key to someone who matches your style. But when you have a few prospects, move forward gently.

Find out as much as you can about the likely mentor and try scheduling a short phone interview by saying you have a few particular questions or generally want information about your brain.

You should travel to them and, particularly

at first, make it as easy for them to help you as you can. At the end of the initial interview, if it seems to have gone well, you can address the idea of speaking again, either over the phone or in person, at some point.

Over time, if they feel receptive, you may come up with the idea of a more conventional mentoring relationship with more particular parameters and goals.

Think about rivalry - Well, not your direct rivalry. For example, if you are in wind sleeve retailing, someone who sells kites is not in direct rivalry with you, but may still have some ideas about the outdoor products industry.

If you have a brick and mortar store, you can

even call someone who does exactly what you do in a faraway place, suppose you are in New York City and they are in Arizona.

However, the web is increasingly putting retailers, even on different continents, in a situation of rivalry, so you have to take a step forward. A different suggestion would be to seek the advice of someone in a larger business than yours who may be less likely to see it as rivalry.

Take advantage of your field - your suppliers, your local chamber of commerce and relevant trade publications are a great source of potential mentors. These are all great places to come for knowledgeable individuals, but how do you find someone who matches your personal style? Look for a mentor the same way people look for medical

professionals, they look for recommendations.

Pay for mentoring - But what if you have an incredible idea that you want to take off quickly, and need a quick jolt of experience? Great informal mentoring is cultivated little by little and can often last for years. If you need an emergency program, it may be time to bring in the consultants.

People at all stages of career progression need coaches to help them. CEOs often use coaches to bounce ideas, entrepreneurs use their coaches to help them think strategically about the business, and coaches help others make career decisions.

Think of the effect it can have in offering to

FROM EMPLOYEE TO ENTREPRENEUR

train your partners, employees and customers. You are able to be a coach for the people around you and help them achieve their goals faster and easier.

Individuals are looking for coaches for 2 basic causes:

- Some individuals are looking for coaches to help them discover a balance between their personal and professional lives.

- Others want coaches to help them be more productive in their business or help them improve their business.

Individuals are no longer looking for quick answers. They are looking for ways to produce lasting change. The traditional consultant does not really produce lasting change. A coach is a kind of consultant who works with clients to create their own lasting change.

Coaching is the next evolutionary stage of consulting. Coaching is a mix of business, finance, psychology, philosophy, transformation and spirituality. It helps people get more out of life than they want, whether it's business success, fiscal independence, academic excellence, personal success, physical well-being, relationships or career planning.

Coaches are resonance boxes, support systems, cheerleaders and teammates all in one. In short, a coach's job is to help others realize their full potential.

Coaches use questioning skills, listening strategies and motivation to help people develop the skills, knowledge and confidence necessary to improve their professional and personal lives.

A coach is a collaborative partner who helps you achieve things. Coaching is not a substitute for personal responsibility and personal choice or alteration.

You need a coach if:

- Your business is not working as well as you want it to.

FROM EMPLOYEE TO ENTREPRENEUR

- You feel like you're working harder and you're less gratified.

- Your business is doing well and you're getting tired of working so hard.

- A large downsizing of your company is causing a big change in the work environment.

- You think your career is approaching a plateau.

- You have an underperformance review.

- You are not capable of shaping and leading your staff.

- It's not easy to draw strategic conclusions.

A coach gives you a place to have a little perspective. A coach is someone who isn't caught up in all the day-to-day things and who can see the big picture.

 FROM EMPLOYEE TO ENTREPRENEUR

Final thoughts

Once I decided to follow up on my business impulses, the conversion from employee to entrepreneur was easier because I initially developed the entrepreneurial spirit while working and used the time to be attentive to situations and formulate the skills I would need to be successful.

You are also capable of making the transition to an entrepreneurial mindset and I trust you will.

Visit our author page on Amazon and get more **MENTES LIBRES!**

http://amazon.com/author/menteslibres

If you wish, you can leave a comment on this book by clicking on the following link so that we can continue to grow! Thank you very much for your purchase!

https://www.amazon.com/dp/B082J3ZL8L

www.ingramcontent.com/pod-product-compliance
Lightning Source LLC
Chambersburg PA
CBHW070837220526
45466CB00002B/806